MINI GUIDE

SPACE

2001 Friedman/Fairfax Publishers

This edition published exclusively for
Friedman/Fairfax Publishing Group.

ISBN 1-5866-3217-5

A Marshall Edition
Conceived, edited, and designed by
Marshall Editions Ltd
The Orangery
161 New Bond Street
London W1S 2UF

99 00 01 02 M 9 8 7 6 5 4 3 2

Copyright © 2000 Marshall
Editions Developments Ltd

Originated in Singapore by Master Image
Printed in Hong Kong by Imago

Distributed by Sterling Publishing
Company, Inc.
387 Park Avenue South
New York, NY 10016
Distributed in Canada by Sterling Publishing
Canadian Manda Group
One Atlantic Avenue, Suite 105
Toronto, Ontario, Canada M6K 3E7

MINI GUIDE
SPACE

Ian Graham

Friedman/Fairfax Publishers

Contents

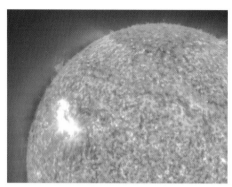

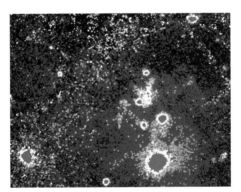

• •

The solar system

The Sun, our nearest star, holds the
solar system together.

Empire of the Sun

The Sun dominates the surrounding space and everything in it, ruling an empire of worlds that includes the Earth, our home planet.

Jupiter

The solar system

The solar system is the name given to the Sun and everything that orbits, or travels around it. This includes the nine major planets and their moons; thousands of asteroids, or minor planets; comets; and countless smaller pieces of rock and tiny particles of matter. The whole system cartwheels through space held together by the immensely powerful pull of the Sun's gravity.

Ma

Earth

Venus

Mercury

How it formed

About 4.6 billion years ago, a cloud of gas and dust in space began to collapse (1). The collapse may have been triggered when a nearby star exploded. The cloud became a rotating disk. Clumps of matter formed in the disk (2). Millions of years later, the Sun burst into life as a star and the surrounding clumps became the planets (3).

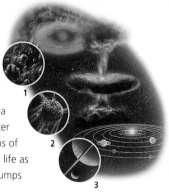

Saturn

Uranus

Neptune

Pluto

The solar orbits

The nine planets orbit the Sun in the same direction but at increasing distances from the Sun. At the same time, each planet spins on its axis (an imaginary line joining a planet's north and south poles).

Pluto's orbit is elongated and tilted to the others

On its long journey around the Sun, Pluto's orbit dips inside that of Neptune, and it becomes closer than Neptune to the Sun

Pluto

Neptune

Uranus

Saturn

Jupiter

Orbits of Mercury, Venus, Earth, and Mars (from center out)

9

Home star

The Sun is a giant ball of hydrogen and helium gas. It is heated by nuclear energy, radiating light and warmth to the solar system.

Facula—an extra bright area with a higher temperature than its surroundings

The Sun's surface

The surface of the Sun, called the photosphere, is not solid like that of the Earth. It is a deep layer of gases with a temperature of around 10,000°F (5,500°C). Above the photosphere, there is a hotter region, the chromosphere. Its temperature increases with height, from 8,000°F (4,500°C) to 180,000°F (100,000°C). Beyond the chromosphere, there is an even hotter region, the corona, with a temperature of 1.8 million °F (1 million °C).

Sunspot

Sunspots

Dark spots often appear on the Sun's surface, each lasting around a week. One sunspot can be bigger than the Earth. Sunspots look darker than the rest of the Sun because they have been cooled by the Sun's intense magnetism.

Prominence—a tongue, or arch, of gas

Sunspot

Partial eclipse

Total eclipse showing solar corona

Diamond-ring effect

Solar eclipse

A solar eclipse happens when the Moon passes between the Earth and the Sun and casts a shadow on the Earth. At the center of the shadow, called the umbra, the whole Sun is hidden behind the Moon, and people on the Earth see a total eclipse. In the rest of the shadow, called the penumbra, people see a partial eclipse.

Moon

Sun

Earth

The Sun is a boiling cauldron of fiery gases, where planet-sized tongues of gas sometimes explode into space.

Flare—a huge explosion on the Sun's surface

Photosphere

Corona

Chromosphere

Spicule—a spikelike explosion

NEVER look directly at the Sun, even when wearing sunglasses. The Sun's intense light could damage your eyes.

Hothouse worlds

Mercury and Venus are the closest planets to the Sun. Tiny Mercury is hard to spot from the Earth because it rises and sets with the Sun, but Venus shines like a bright star at dawn and dusk.

Rocky Mercury

Mercury is a small, rocky, and heavily cratered world. By day, its surface is baked by the Sun, reaching a temperature of up to 800°F (427°C). At night, without any atmosphere to spread the Sun's heat around the planet, the surface temperature plummets to −297°F (−183°C).

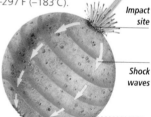

Impact site

Shock waves

Impact craters

Mercury is covered with craters. The biggest, the Caloris Basin, is 775 miles (1,250 kilometers) across. Shock waves from the impact that caused it spread all the way through the planet, breaking up the surface on its opposite side.

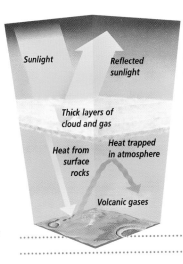

Greenhouse planet

Venus is permanently cloaked in thick layers of cloud and gas. The small amount of sunlight that manages to get through warms the surface. Most of the heat cannot escape back into space through the thick clouds. The heat builds up and up, giving Venus a surface temperature of more than 900°F (480°C).

Sunlight

Reflected sunlight

Thick layers of cloud and gas

Heat from surface rocks

Heat trapped in atmosphere

Volcanic gases

The surface of Venus

The surface of Venus is an extremely hostile place. Clouds contain drops of sulfuric acid, which turn the sky yellow. The thick atmosphere creates a crushing surface pressure 90 times greater than that on the Earth. The temperature is high enough to melt lead. Venus has fewer visible craters than Mercury or the Moon because they have been covered by lava from its many volcanoes.

Bright blue gem

The Earth is like no other place in the universe. As far as we know, it is the only place where life exists. We have life on the Earth because of the combination of heat, light, and water found here.

World of water and life

The Earth is the only planet in the solar system with liquid water on its surface. Life on the Earth began in this water around 4 billion years ago. Early sea creatures and plants used carbon dioxide from the atmosphere and released oxygen, slowly creating the atmosphere we have today.

Water means life, as shown in this image (right) of lush vegetation around the Nile Delta, Egypt.

About three-quarters of the Earth's surface is covered with water. Water helps to create the Earth's changing weather patterns.

Our home planet

The Earth is an active planet. It is always changing. The crust of rock at the surface floats on top of liquid rock, which, in turn, surrounds a metal core at the center of the planet. The Earth's crust is divided into huge plates that constantly jostle and move against one another. This movement can cause volcanoes and earthquakes, which can dramatically reshape the Earth's surface, building new land from lava flows or opening up huge cracks in the ground.

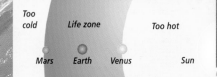

The life zone

Life as we know it can exist only where there is liquid water. Planets close to the Sun are too hot for water to exist as a liquid—it boils and evaporates into space. Planets far from the Sun are too cold—water freezes. The Earth orbits the Sun in the middle of the "life zone." It is the only planet with liquid water

15

The Moon

Sun's light

The Moon is the Earth's closest neighbor in space. It was formed around 4.6 billion years ago from rock blasted into space when the Earth was hit by an object as big as the planet Mars.

An airless world

The Moon is a small, dusty, and airless world. Its gravity is weak—too weak to hold onto any gases that it may have had in the past. Because it has no air or liquid water, it has no weather to alter its surface. Its mountains, craters, and dusty landscape have therefore hardly changed for billions of years.

SEA OF COLD
Plato
SEA OF SERENITY
SEA OF RAINS
SEA OF CRISES
Aristarchus
Mountains
SEA OF VAPORS
SEA OF TRANQUILITY
SEA OF FERTILITY
Eratosthenes
Copernicus
Kepler
Ptolemaeus
Alphonsus
Langrenus
SEA OF NECTAR
OCEAN OF STORMS
Arzachel
Grimaldi
SEA OF CLOUDS
SEA OF MOISTURE
Tycho

Some of the main features on the Moon's surface can be seen from the Earth with binoculars.

The Moon always shows the same face to the Earth because it spins once on its axis in the same time that it takes to orbit the Earth—once every 27.3 days.

16

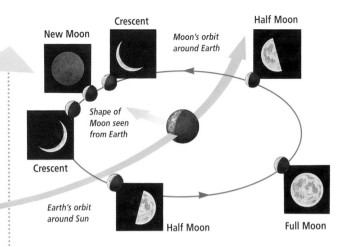

New Moon

Crescent

Moon's orbit around Earth

Half Moon

Shape of Moon seen from Earth

Crescent

Earth's orbit around Sun

Half Moon

Full Moon

Moon phases and eclipses

As the Moon circles the Earth and as the Earth orbits the Sun, we see different parts of the Moon lit up by the Sun. The different shapes of the Moon we see from the Earth are called the phases of the Moon. Sometimes the Sun, Earth, and Moon line up so that the Earth casts a shadow on the Moon. The result is a partial or total lunar eclipse.

Moon   Earth   Sun

Craters

The Moon's surface is littered with thousands of shallow holes called craters, caused by rocks hurtling into it from space. Some craters are hundreds of miles across. Most are smaller. Eratosthenes (right) is 36 miles (58 kilometers) wide.

The red planet

Seen from Earth, Mars shines blood red in the night sky, almost twice as bright as the nearest star.

Mariner Valley

Martians?

Mars is the only planet in the solar system with surface markings that can be seen easily from the Earth. At the beginning of the 20th century, some astronomers believed, wrongly, that marks they saw on the surface of Mars were evidence of intelligent life.

A deep crack, called the Mariner Valley, stretches a quarter of the way around Mars.

Water on Mars?

There are signs that water may once have flowed on Mars. Some of the planet's surface features look like dried-up riverbeds and flood plains. A global change in climate 3 billion years ago drove off most of the water, leaving some ice at the poles and under the surface.

Image of dried-up water channels on Mars

Dried-up riverbed

Ice clouds

Crater

Recent visitors

In July 1997, the *Pathfinder* space probe
landed on Mars. A miniature rover called
Sojourner trundled out of the lander and
explored the Martian surface for three
months. In the same year, the *Mars Global
Surveyor* went into orbit around Mars and began
mapping its surface with cameras, lasers, and radar.

Sojourner
**exploring the
Martian surface**

The Martian surface

Mars looks red because it is covered with reddish, iron-rich dust.
The dust is blown around the planet by winds. The highlands are
covered with craters, while large parts of the
lower regions have been smoothed by lava
flows. Daily temperatures on the surface
range from −128°F (−89°C) to −24°F (−31°C).

Volcano

Dust storm

Thin atmosphere

Mist

The gas giant

Jupiter is the biggest planet in the solar system and heavier than all the other planets put together. It is made of hydrogen—the gas that fuels all stars—but never grew big enough to become a star itself.

The Great Red Spot

The biggest feature visible on Jupiter is its Great Red Spot, a violent storm large enough to hold two Earths side by side. The spot stands out clearly against the light and dark cloud bands that cross the planet. The storm was seen for the first time more than 300 years ago and it still rages. It has been able to last so long because Jupiter has no solid surface to weaken the storm's energy.

Dark clouds left by the impact of comet Shoemaker–Levy 9

Fragments of comet Shoemaker-Levy 9 hurtling toward Jupiter

Comet collision

In July 1994, Jupiter was struck by a comet. The comet, called Shoemaker-Levy 9, had been torn apart by Jupiter's gravity into a string of rocky fragments. When they hit the planet, they caused fireballs, which left huge black and brown stains visible in Jupiter's cloud-tops for months.

Jupiter's moons

Jupiter has 16 moons. Four of them— Callisto, Ganymede, Europa, and Io—were discovered in 1610 when the astronomer Galileo looked at Jupiter through a telescope for the first time. Callisto is as big as the planet Mercury. Ganymede is the solar system's largest moon; Io is its most volcanic world. Europa may have an ocean of water under its icy surface.

Europa

Io

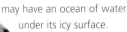

Callisto

Ganymede

21

Disk world

Saturn, surrounded by its broad, flat disk of rings, is the most easily recognizable of the nine planets in the solar system. Saturn is a gas giant, like Jupiter, and is nearly as big.

Rings of ice

Although Saturn's rings look solid, they are made up of billions of pieces of ice-covered rock. The smallest are mere specks of dust, while the largest are probably as big as houses. Some may even be half a mile (1 kilometer) wide. Each piece of rock travels in its own orbit around Saturn.

The pieces of icy rock orbiting Saturn could once have been a moon or they may be material left over from Saturn's formation.

Saturn's moons

Saturn has at least 18 moons. The largest, Titan, is the only moon known to have a thick atmosphere. Enceladus has a cratered part and a much smoother part. Mimas has a huge crater made by an impact that nearly shattered it.

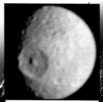
Mimas

Enceladus

Saturn
D ring
C ring
Bright B ring

Cassini Division—gap filled with faint ringlets

A ring

F ring

G ring

E ring

Rings within rings

Saturn appears to be surrounded by just a few broad rings, but there are actually thousands of narrow rings and ringlets. The ringlets that make up the narrow F ring are twisted together and kept separate from the other rings by the gravity of two nearby "shepherd" moons, called Prometheus and Pandora.

Hazy blue Uranus

The gas giant Uranus is four times the size of the Earth. It orbits the Sun lying on one side because the axis on which it spins is tilted.

Rings ranging from (1 mile) (1.5 km) wide for the inner ring to between 12 and 60 miles (20 and 96 km) wide for the outer ring

Rings of Uranus

Nine dark rings around Uranus were discovered by accident in 1977. Astronomers noticed that a star dimmed several times as Uranus passed in front of it and realized that rings around Uranus must have obscured it. Another two rings were discovered by the *Voyager 2* space probe in 1986.

Image of Uranus from the *Hubble Space Telescope*

Rings made up of black particles

Moons of Uranus

Uranus has at least 17 moons. They range in size from tiny Cordelia, only 16 miles (26 kilometers) wide, to Titania, 980 miles (1,578 kilometers) wide. All the moons have craters but Miranda, at 293 mile (472 kilometers) wide, is also covered with thousands of trenches and long canyons. Because Uranus is tilted on its axis, its moons look as though they are circling the planet's poles. In fact, they are orbiting its equator.

Miranda

Under the cloud-tops

Hazy white clouds made of frozen crystals of methane gas float up to 30 miles (50 kilometers) above Neptune's main blue cloud layers. Below, the atmosphere is made up of hydrogen, helium, and methane gases. The methane clouds give Uranus its distinctive blue-green color.

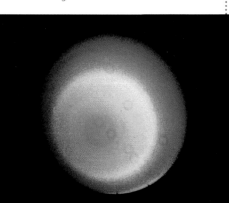

Enhanced *Hubble* image showing high-altitude haze over Uranus's south pole

Stormy Neptune

Neptune was discovered in 1845, but it remained a mystery until *Voyager 2* flew past it in 1989. *Voyager*'s photographs showed Neptune's bright blue methane atmosphere with ice-white clouds.

The Great Dark Spot

In 1989, *Voyager 2* photographed a giant storm on Neptune named the Great Dark Spot. Winds raced around it at 1,250 miles (2,000 kilometers) per hour—the fastest recorded winds in the solar system. The Great Dark Spot looked like Jupiter's Great Red Spot but it was not as long-lasting. When the *Hubble Space Telescope* photographed Neptune again, in 1994, the storm had disappeared.

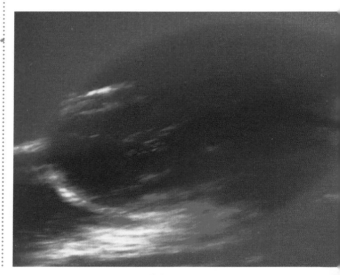

1994

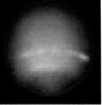

1995

Stormy weather

Scientists had thought that Neptune would be a cold, still world because it is so far from the Sun. However, images from the *Hubble Space Telescope* show changing weather patterns and storms in Neptune's atmosphere which must be driven by heat from within the planet.

1996

Changing cloud patterns on Neptune taken by the *Hubble Space Telescope*

Moons of Neptune

Neptune has at least eight moons. Six were discovered by *Voyager 2* in 1989. The largest is Triton. When *Voyager* photographed it, Triton's south pole had a pinkish color, probably caused by frozen nitrogen. Liquid nitrogen vaporizes and bursts through Triton's surface as geysers 19 miles (30 kilometers) high. Dust falling from these geysers makes dark streaks across the moon's surface.

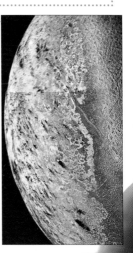

Triton

Triton's surface

Geyser

Pluto and the minor planets

Thousands of pieces of rock left over from the formation of the solar system orbit the Sun. Pluto may not be a planet at all but one of these asteroids, or minor planets.

Pluto and Charon

Pluto is the smallest planet. For most of the time, it is also the most distant planet from the Sun. Scientists think that Pluto may be one of many icy worlds that orbit the Sun beyond Neptune in the Kuiper Belt. Pluto (see top right in this Hubble photograph) has one moon, called Charon. Charon, at about half its size, is unusually large compared to Pluto.

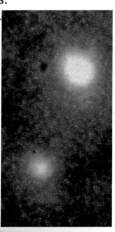

Charon (left) and the Sun (center), as seen from Pluto's surface

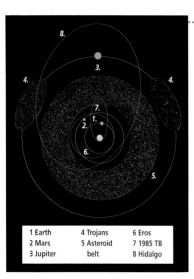

1 Earth
2 Mars
3 Jupiter
4 Trojans
5 Asteroid belt
6 Eros
7 1985 TB
8 Hidalgo

The asteroid belt

Most asteroids orbit the Sun in a wide belt between the orbits of Mars and Jupiter. Two groups of asteroids, called the Trojans, orbit with Jupiter. One group is ahead of Jupiter; the other is behind.

Some asteroids, such as Eros, travel closer to the Sun than others in the asteroid belt. Hidalgo has a long, looping orbit.

Minor planets

More than 9,000 asteroids have been tracked and named. In 1991, as it passed through the asteroid belt on its way to Jupiter, the *Galileo* spacecraft took the first-ever close-up photographs of an asteroid—Gaspra. In 1993, *Galileo* photographed Ida, the first asteroid discovered to have its own moon, called Dactyl. Mathilde was photographed in 1997 by the *Near Earth Asteroid Rendezvous* spacecraft. These three asteroids are all pitted with craters where they have been hit by smaller rocks.

1 Gaspra—15 km (9 miles) long
2 Mathilde—66 km (41 miles) long
3 Ida—56 km (35 miles) long

Cosmic snowballs

A bright comet with a glowing head and a long tail is one of the most amazing sights in the night sky.

Dust tail

Coma
(surrounding
nucleus)

Gas tail

The comet's nucleus

A comet is a lump of rock and snow, called the nucleus, surrounded by a cloud of gas and dust, called the coma. Although the nucleus is very small, often only about 6 miles (10 kilometers) across, the coma can be bigger than the planet Jupiter. No one had seen a comet's nucleus until the *Giotto* spacecraft took close-up photographs of Halley's Comet in 1986. Images show a dark rock measuring 5 by 9 miles (8 by 15 kilometers), with bright jets of gas spurting out of its surface on the side facing the Sun.

Giotto and (above) its image of Halley's Comet

Comet Hale-
Bopp visible
from Earth in 1997

Dust and gas

A comet's coma and tails
glow, but they give out no light
of their own. Their glow is reflected
sunlight. Comet dust is rich in carbon
and silicon. Comet gas is mostly water
vapor. Sunlight breaks it down and
produces enormous hydrogen clouds tens
of millions of miles across.

Evolution of a comet's tail

For most of its orbit around the Sun, a comet nucleus has no tail.
As it approaches the Sun, it warms up. Snow on its surface vaporizes,
releasing gas and dust into space. Sunlight and the solar wind
(particles from the Sun) sweep the gas and dust into two tails—a
whitish dust tail and a blue gas tail. Both point away from the Sun.

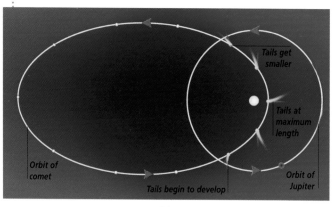

Tails get
smaller

Tails at
maximum
length

Orbit of
comet

Orbit of
Jupiter

Tails begin to develop

Shooting stars

Look up at night and you may be lucky enough to see a light streaking across the sky. It lasts a moment and then it is gone. We call these streaks of light shooting stars, but they are not real stars.

What is a shooting star?

Space contains billions of pieces of rock and dust hurtling about at great speed. Most of these meteoroids are as small as a speck of dust or a grain of sand and cannot be seen from the Earth. However, if one of them collides with the air particles in the Earth's atmosphere, it heats up and glows white hot, forming the streak of light, or shooting star, we see from the ground. A moment later, it is vaporized by the intense heat and disappears.

Meteor shower

Meteor streams

There are more shooting stars, or meteors, on some nights of the year than others. Streams of shooting stars that occur on the same nights each year are called meteor showers. As a comet travels around the Sun, it leaves a trail of dust particles, or a meteor stream, around its whole orbit. We see yearly meteor showers when the Earth passes through this dust tail.

Meteor stream (comet's dust trail)

Sun

Earth

Earth's orbit

What are they made of?

It is difficult to study meteoroids because most burn up in the Earth's atmosphere before they hit the ground. Large meteoroids that reach the Earth are called meteorites. There are three main types of meteorites: stones, irons, and stony-irons. Stone meteorites are the most common. Irons are made of iron and nickel. Stony-irons are a mixture of stone and iron.

Iron meteorite

Stony-iron meteorite

Stars and galaxies

New stars are being born all the time in vast, cold clouds of interstellar gas and dust.

Star birth

In the night sky, stars look like constant, unchanging points of light, but they are not. New stars are forming all the time. They are born in vast, dark clouds of cold gas and dust called nebulae.

What is a star?

A star is a dazzlingly bright ball of glowing gas. The gas, which is mostly hydrogen, is not burning like a fire. The star is such a massive object that it has an enormously strong force of gravity pulling toward its center. The crushing pressure at the center is so powerful that the particles of hydrogen smash together and form a different element, helium. In the process, called nuclear fusion, energy is released. It is this energy that makes a star shine, sometimes for billions of years.

Clusters of stars forming in columns of cold gas in the Eagle Nebula

1 A cluster of bright new stars emerges from a cloud of gas and dust.

2 Hot gas from the stars triggers the formation of more stars in the cloud.

3 A second cluster of stars emerges and triggers more star formation.

Stellar nurseries

Stars rarely form on their own but in clusters. Clumps of gas inside a nebula start to fall in on themselves because of their gravity, attracting more and more gas from the nebula. As they become more massive, they heat up until nuclear fusion starts and the new stars burst into life.

Orion Nebula

The nearest bright nebula in which we can see newly formed stars is the Orion Nebula. The *Hubble Space Telescope* has taken photographs of young stars in the Orion Nebula surrounded by gas and dust that may form planets.

Orion Nebula

A star's life

Stars develop over millions of years. The way they age and how long they last depend on their mass—the amount of material they contain.

Sun

Giant stars

The Sun is bigger than many stars in our galaxy, but it is dwarfed by giant and supergiant stars. Blue giants are young hot stars that may be 15 times the size of the Sun. Red giants are old stars near the end of their life that can become as big as 100 Suns. The biggest stars of all are the supergiants. A supergiant can be up to 1,000 times the size of the Sun.

Red dwarf

White dwarf

Brown dwarf

Dwarf stars

Dwarf stars are the smallest stars in the universe. White dwarfs are old stars. They are about the same size as the Earth but they contain as much matter as the Sun. They continue cooling until they become a cold black cinder. Red dwarfs are faint young stars that are cooler and smaller in size and mass than the Sun. Some stars with a small mass do not get hot enough to start nuclear fusion (see page 36). They are cool stars that glow faintly and are called brown dwarfs.

Sun

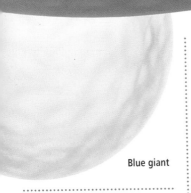

Red supergiant

Blue giant

Star colors

Stars are classified according to color as well as size. Red stars are the coolest. Hotter stars are yellow, and the hottest stars are bluish white. Our Sun is a yellow star. On a clear night, it is possible to see bright white and orange stars from the Earth.

Bright blue-white stars in the Pleiades, or Seven Sisters, cluster

Variable stars

Variable stars grow brighter then dimmer, again and again. A star can vary, or change, like this when a dim, orbiting companion star passes in front of it. Other stars, called pulsating variables, change in brightness as they grow and shrink in a regular cycle.

Pulsating star cycle

3 Star at its biggest; starts to cool
4 Star starts to shrink; at its coolest
5 Star at its smallest; starts to expand

1 Star begins to expand
2 Star at its brightest and hottest

Dying stars

Star becomes
a red giant

**Stars change color and size as they age.
Eventually, they die. A star only lasts as long
as it has fuel to burn. Even our Sun will one
day die, but not for another 5 billion years.**

A star like our Sun
shines for about
10 billion years. For
most of the time, it
is a yellow star, like
the Sun is now.

*Large blue
star*

*Gas and dust blown off
giant stars and in supernova
explosions mix into the
interstellar clouds, where
new generations of stars
are born*

A blue star 10 times
the mass and at
least 3 times as big
as the Sun shines
for around 30
million years.

Blue giant

Collapsing stars

*Blue giant gets bigger,
cooler, and redder*

Heat makes a star grow bigger,
while gravity tries to make it smaller.
They are in balance until the star runs out of fuel and begins
to cool. Gravity takes over and the star collapses. What happens
next depends on the star's mass (how much material it contains).
A star like the Sun heats up as its core shrinks. The heat pushes its
outer layers outward, forming a cool red giant star. It then throws
off shells of gas until only the core is left, leaving a white dwarf.
A star with 10 times the Sun's fuel forms a cool red supergiant.
When it runs out of fuel, it collapses in less than a second, blowing
itself apart in a violent explosion called a supernova.

40

White dwarf gradually cools and fades

Core remains as white dwarf

Red giant blows off its outer layers of gas

Black holes

If the core left when a giant star blows itself to bits is less massive than three Suns, it forms an object called a neutron star. If the core is more massive, nothing can stop its total collapse and it forms a black hole. Its gravity is so powerful that nothing, not even light, can escape from its surface.

Star becomes a red supergiant

Supernova explosion

Collapsed core becomes a neutron star or black hole

Crab Nebula

In the year 1054, astronomers in China saw an intensely bright light appear in the sky. It was a supernova explosion. We can see its remains today as the Crab Nebula. At its center, there is a tiny neutron star spinning 30 times every second.

Patterns in the sky

People have seen patterns in the stars for thousands of years. We still use them today to find our way round the sky.

Exploring the sky

The thousands of stars visible in the night sky are divided into 88 patterns called constellations. Astronomers of the ancient world named 48 constellations. Another 40 were added later. You can explore the sky by learning to find one or two well-known constellations and using them as markers or signposts to find others.

The Pleiades

Orion (the hunter) is one of the easiest constellations to find because of the three bright stars forming a line through its middle, representing the hunter's belt. From Orion, it is easy to trace a line to other nearby constellations.

Castor

Pollux   GEMINI

Aldebaran   TAURUS

CANIS MINOR   Betelgeuse

Procyon

ORION

Rigel

Sirius

CANIS MAJOR   LEPUS   ERIDANUS

Star distances

The stars that make up a constellation look as if they are close to each other in space. In fact, some of them are much closer to us than others. They appear close together because they lie in the same direction when viewed from the Earth. The stars in the Orion constellation range from a couple of hundred light-years to more than 1,000 light-years from the Earth.

Distances of stars making up Orion

Heka

Betelgeuse

Alnilam

Mintaka

Bellatrix

Orion Nebula

Alnitak

Nair Al Saif

Saiph

Rigel

Line of vision

1,500   1,250   1,000   750   500   250   0
Light-years from Earth

Star Charts

Modern star charts still use the names of the constellations given by ancient Greek and Arabic astronomers. Long ago, many star maps would have had drawings around the star patterns, such as the figure of Orion, the hunter. Modern maps simply show lines joining the stars in the constellation.

Nearly all the brightest stars have names. Many also have a Greek letter (such as alpha or beta) or a number.

ecliptic

+20°

GEMINI

TAURUS

Aldebaran

ORION

+10°

Betelgeuse   32   Bellatrix

M78

0°

Orion
Nebula
M43/M42

ERIDANUS

29   Rigel

-10°

MONOCEROS   LEPUS

43

Galaxies

Stars are not spread evenly through space. They are grouped together in galaxies.

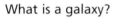

What is a galaxy?

A galaxy is an unimaginably large group of stars moving through space, held together by the pull of gravity.

NGC 2997 spiral galaxy

Astronomers have found billions of galaxies. The smallest contain millions of stars. The largest have thousands of billions of stars.

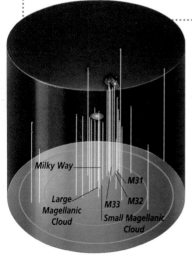

Two irregular galaxies—the Large and Small Magellanic clouds—orbit the Milky Way.

The Local Group

Our own star, the Sun, belongs to a galaxy called the Milky Way. The Milky Way belongs to a cluster of about 30 galaxies called the Local Group. Its three largest members are the Milky Way, the Andromeda Galaxy (M31), and M33. The Local Group lies near the edge of a larger cluster of about 400 galaxies. These, and others, form a supercluster, called the Local Supercluster.

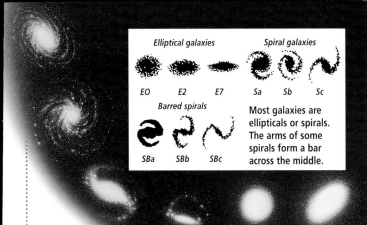

| Elliptical galaxies | | | Spiral galaxies | | |
| E0 | E2 | E7 | Sa | Sb | Sc |

Barred spirals

| SBa | SBb | SBc |

Most galaxies are ellipticals or spirals. The arms of some spirals form a bar across the middle.

Galaxy types

Galaxies come in a wide range of shapes and sizes. In the 1920s, the astronomer Edwin Hubble divided them up into four basic shapes—elliptical (E), spiral (S), barred spiral (SB), and irregular (I). He then added numbers and letters to show how flat an elliptical galaxy is or whether a spiral galaxy's arms were tightly wound or more open.

Unusual galaxies

Some galaxies form odd shapes. The small galaxy (top right) crashed through the galaxy pictured below it. The collision set off star formation. The new stars appear as the bright ring of light (left), like a wheel.

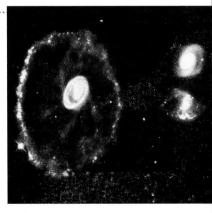

Cartwheel Galaxy

45

The Milky Way

The solar system lies in part of the Milky Way Galaxy. When you look up into the night sky, all the stars you can see, and millions more besides, belong to the Milky Way.

Our galaxy

The Milky Way is a spiral galaxy containing more than 200 billion stars. The main disk of the galaxy is around 2,000 light-years thick and 100,000 light-years across. The Sun lies 25,000 light-years from the galaxy's center in one of its spiral arms, the Orion arm.

The Milky Way looks like a hazy band of light when viewed from the Earth (above).

Milky Way cross-section

If we could travel out into space and look back at the Milky Way edge-on, it would look like a thin disk (1) with a layer of dust running through it (2) and a bright bulge in the center (3). The central bulge is about 6,000 light-years thick and 15,000 light-years across. Globular star clusters (4) surround the galaxy, forming a round halo (5). These clusters formed early in the galaxy's history and contain the Milky Way's oldest stars. Their position suggests that our galaxy was once shaped like a ball. The whole galaxy rotates. The Sun takes about 220 million years to travel around the center of the galaxy.

Thick gas and dust surround the center of the Milky Way, preventing us from seeing what lies there. Some astronomers think it may be a black hole.

Active galaxies

Some galaxies produce huge amounts of light or radio energy. Astronomers believe these "active galaxies" may be powered by huge black holes at their centers.

Radio galaxies

Active galaxies were first discovered in the 1940s. Astronomers found that some distant galaxies were giving out more energy as radio waves than as light waves. This type of active galaxy is also called a radio galaxy. Most of the radio waves are from two giant jets or clouds of matter coming out of the center of the galaxy rather than from the galaxy itself. The only power source known today that could drive this immense outpouring of energy is a giant black hole.

Energy given off

Black hole

Rotating disk of matter

Radio cloud

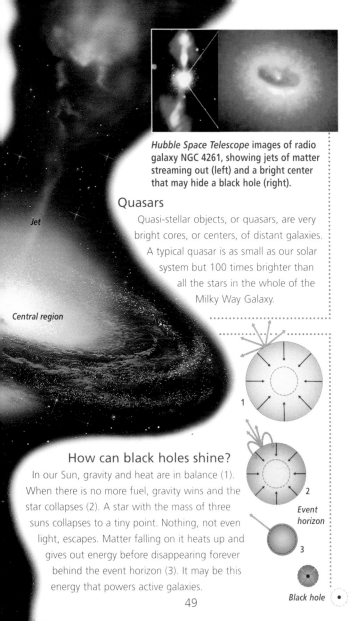

Hubble Space Telescope images of radio galaxy NGC 4261, showing jets of matter streaming out (left) and a bright center that may hide a black hole (right).

Jet

Central region

Quasars

Quasi-stellar objects, or quasars, are very bright cores, or centers, of distant galaxies. A typical quasar is as small as our solar system but 100 times brighter than all the stars in the whole of the Milky Way Galaxy.

1

2

Event horizon

3

Black hole

How can black holes shine?

In our Sun, gravity and heat are in balance (1). When there is no more fuel, gravity wins and the star collapses (2). A star with the mass of three suns collapses to a tiny point. Nothing, not even light, escapes. Matter falling on it heats up and gives out energy before disappearing forever behind the event horizon (3). It may be this energy that powers active galaxies.

49

The Big Bang

Our universe came into being about 15 billion years ago. All of time and space appeared from a tiny point called a singularity in the biggest explosion ever—the Big Bang.

The Big Bang

The new universe was small and very hot at first, but it expanded fast. As it grew in size, it began to cool. As it cooled, some of its energy changed into matter: at first hydrogen, then helium, then other elements.

Protogalaxies form

Hydrogen and helium form

Gas clouds cool

Big Bang explosion

TIME

Big Bang + 3 minutes

Big Bang + 1 million years

Big Bang + 1 billion years

Formation of the universe

The matter that formed within the first second after the Big Bang flew out in all directions. Where there is matter, there is also gravity. Gravity pulled the matter together. Within 300,000 years, swirling clouds of gas had formed. In another million years, the clouds were contracting due to their own gravity, forming spinning clumps called protogalaxies—the first stage of galaxy formation.

Cosmic ripples

In 1989, the *Cosmic Background Explorer (COBE)* satellite was launched to study the energy left over from the Big Bang. *COBE*'s map of this energy showed ripples that represent differences in the temperature of the early universe.

First galaxies form

Large galaxies form

Big Bang + 3 billion years

Big Bang + 5 billion years

Early galaxies

Inside protogalaxies, clumps of gas formed the first stars, transforming protogalaxies into galaxies. Then, 5 billion years after the Big Bang, the solar system formed inside the Milky Way Galaxy.

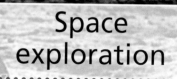

Space exploration

U.S. astronaut Buzz Aldrin walking on the
dusty surface of the Moon

Telescopes

Astronomers have explored the universe with telescopes since the beginning of the 17th century. Today's telescopes are huge and extremely sensitive.

Reflecting telescope

Eyepiece

Secondary mirror

Path of light

Dish-shaped main mirror

Refracting telescope

Path of light

Main lens

Eyepiece

Optical telescopes

There are two types of optical, or light-collecting, telescopes—reflectors and refractors. A reflector uses mirrors; a refractor uses lenses. Light enters a reflector through its open end, travels down the telescope, and bounces off the main, or primary, mirror. A small secondary mirror sends the light out through the eyepiece. Light enters a refractor through the main lens, or objective, travels down the telescope, and emerges through the eyepiece.

Keck 2

Keck 1

The summit of Mauna Kea in Hawaii, at 13,780 ft (4,200 m) above sea level, is one of the best places on Earth for astronomy because of the clear, steady air. The nine telescopes built there since the 1960s include the world's biggest optical telescopes: Keck 1 and Keck 2.

How telescopes are used

Astronomers rarely look through a telescope's eyepiece. Instead, light collected by the telescope is recorded on computer, then used to produce images. By studying the different colors of light in starlight, astronomers can tell what a star is made from. The Earth keeps turning while astronomers are making their observations. Because of this, a computer also controls the telescope, constantly moving it so that it keeps pointing to the same object in space.

Optical telescope on Mauna Kea

Clear skies

Swirling air currents bend light rays, making stars twinkle and therefore hard to study. Streetlight and light from homes also get into telescopes. For these reasons, large optical telescopes are built in high places where the cool, thin air forms a barrier, holding unstable polluted air currents below.

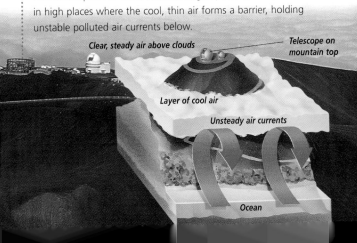

Clear, steady air above clouds

Telescope on mountain top

Layer of cool air

Unsteady air currents

Ocean

Invisible waves

Astronomers have learned a lot about stars by studying the different kinds of energy they give out as well as starlight.

Radio image of three volcanoes in the southern hemisphere of Venus

Radio astronomy

The Earth's atmosphere blocks out most of the energy that arrives from space. Only light and some radio waves pass through the atmosphere and reach the ground. Radio astronomy is a branch of science that uses dish-shaped aerials to pick up radio waves from space and make maps and pictures of the objects that sent them out. Big dishes produce more detailed images than small dishes. Radio dishes in different places on Earth can be linked together electronically so that they act like one enormous dish.

Ultraviolet

Ultraviolet radiation is given out by very hot stars, but is blocked by the ozone layer high in the Earth's atmosphere. Ultraviolet telescopes flown on satellites are used to find young, hot stars.

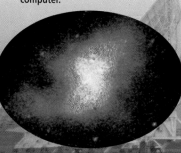

As X-rays are colorless, colors in this X-ray image of Supernova 1987a have been added by computer.

Infrared

Infrared telescopes are used to collect infrared waves from planets and galaxies and also to detect objects, such as nebulae, that cannot be seen in visible light but shine brightly in infrared.

Areas of star birth (bright yellow ring)

Nucleus

Andromeda Galaxy as an infrared image

Andromeda as a visible light image

The Very Large Array is a group of 27 movable radio telescopes in New Mexico. Each telescope dish is 82 ft (25 m) wide.

Eye in the sky

The best place for a telescope is in space, because there is no atmosphere to distort the view of the stars. Space telescopes send their pictures and data back to Earth by radio.

Hubble Space Telescope

The *Hubble Space Telescope (HST)*, placed in orbit in 1990, is the biggest space telescope. It is 43 feet (13 meters) long by 13 feet (4 meters) across and weighs 11 tons (11 tonnes), and its main mirror is over 7 feet (2 meters) wide. The *HST* can detect objects 50 times fainter than any telescope on Earth. The electricity needed to power its cameras, instruments, computers, guidance system, and radio equipment is generated by two solar panels containing 48,000 solar cells. Batteries supply electricity while the telescope passes through the Earth's shadow.

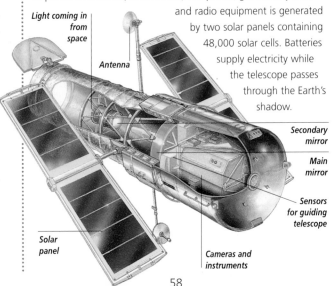

Light coming in from space

Antenna

Secondary mirror

Main mirror

Sensors for guiding telescope

Solar panel

Cameras and instruments

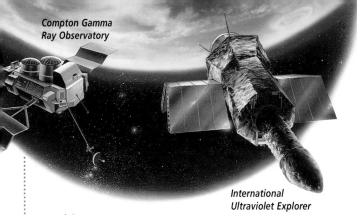

Compton Gamma Ray Observatory

International Ultraviolet Explorer

In orbit

Dozens of telescopes have been launched into orbit around the Earth. The *Compton Gamma Ray Observatory (CGRO)* was launched in 1991. *The International Ultraviolet Explorer (IUE),* launched in 1978, was a very successful telescope because it continued working for 18 years.

NGST

The *Next Generation Space Telescope (NGST),* is now being designed and should be launched by about the year 2007. It will study the first stars and galaxies that formed in the young universe. To create an image from such distant and faint

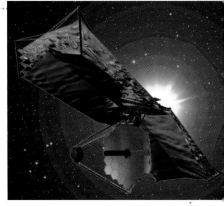

objects, its main mirror will need to be at least 26 feet (8 meters) across, or more than three times that of the *Hubble Space Telescope*. It should be able to study objects 400 times fainter than can be studied with the most powerful telescopes on Earth.

Rockets

A spacecraft has to reach a speed of 5 miles (8 kilometers) per second to escape the pull of Earth's gravity and go into orbit around the Earth. The only engine today that can do this is the rocket.

Rocket pioneers

Many of the rockets that launched early Soviet and American spacecraft were designed by teams led by two brilliant engineers, Sergei Korolev in the U.S.S.R. and Wernher von Braun in the U.S.A. Von Braun developed the V2 rocket in the 1940s, then went on to design the *Saturn 5* Moon rocket. Korolev led teams that put the first man in space and sent probes to the Moon, Mars, and Venus.

Korolev's Zemiorka R7 rocket

Von Braun's V2 rocket

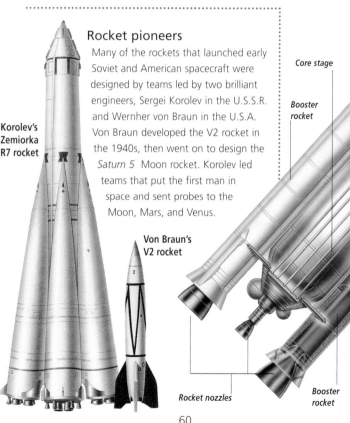

Core stage

Booster rocket

Rocket nozzles

Booster rocket

Upper stage

Ariane 5

Fairing (streamlined casing)

Payload (the rocket's cargo)

The view from an *Ariane 5* rocket as it soars into orbit

The staged rocket

A rocket is made from two or three sections called stages stacked on top of each other. Each stage has its own fuel and rocket engines. As each stage uses up its fuel, it falls away to save weight. Extra rockets called boosters may be added to provide extra thrust. The European *Ariane 5* rocket has two stages. The lower core stage is attached to two booster rockets. When the boosters and core fall away, the upper stage carries the payload into orbit.

Sputnik 1

The first satellite

The first artificial satellite was *Sputnik 1*, launched by the Soviet Union on October 4, 1957. The satellite was a hollow metal ball weighing 185 pounds (84 kilograms) containing a radio transmitter. It re-entered and burned up in the atmosphere on January 4, 1958.

The space race

When the Soviet Union sent the first person into space, it started a space race with the United States that led to 12 American astronauts landing on the Moon.

First man in space

The first spaceman was a Soviet Air Force pilot called Yuri Gagarin. He made one orbit of the Earth in the *Vostok 1* space capsule on April 12, 1961. The capsule was only 8 feet (2.5 meters) across, covered with a heat-shielding material to protect it from the searing temperature of reentry. After reentry, at a height of 22,966 feet (7,000 meters), Gagarin was ejected from the capsule and landed by parachute. The whole flight was over in less than two hours. Gagarin became world-famous overnight.

Launch of *Vostok 1* (top right); the capsule landed separately by parachute (right).

Mercury and Gemini

The United States started a crewed space program three weeks after Gagarin's flight with six one-man Mercury spacecraft flights. These were followed by 10 two-man Gemini flights that practiced the maneuvers needed to land on the Moon.

Gemini

The Apollo Program

The three-man Apollo spacecraft made its first flight in orbit around Earth in October 1968. In December 1968, *Apollo 8* became the first crewed spacecraft to orbit the Moon. After two more test flights, *Apollo 11* made its historic Moon landing in July 1969. Five more successful landings followed.

Saturn 5 launch rocket

Moon 3

Command module **Service module breaks away** 4

After blastoff (1), the Apollo spacecraft headed for the Moon (2). The lunar module landed two of the astronauts on the Moon (3). All three astronauts returned to Earth in the command and cervice modules (4). Only the command module splashed down in the sea (5).

5   1

2

Launch rocket

The lunar module landed on the Moon (A) then used its base as a launching pad to take off (B)

A

B

Space stations

While most crewed space missions last for only a few days or weeks before the spacecraft has to return to Earth, space stations can stay in orbit for years.

Laboratories and living quarters

Computer-generated image showing an early stage in building the *ISS*

Solar panels

International Space Station

Sixteen countries are building a new *International Space Station (ISS)*. It will be the biggest structure ever built in space. The first part was launched by Russia in 1998. The rest will not be completed until at least 2004, after 45 launches of Russian rockets and U.S. space shuttles. Up to seven people will live and work on board the *ISS*, orbiting 217 miles (350 kilometers) above the Earth. Russian Soyuz spacecraft and U.S. space shuttles will be able to dock with it.

The first space stations

The first space station was *Salyut 1*, launched by the Soviet Union in 1971. There were seven Salyut space stations. The U.S. space station, *Skylab*, was made from leftover Moon-rocket parts and launched in 1973. The Soviet Union followed Salyut with *Mir*, launched in 1986 and crewed until 1999.

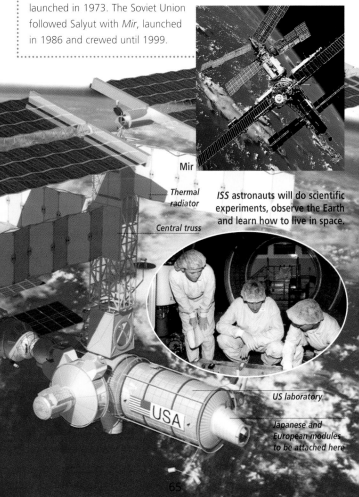

Mir

Thermal radiator

ISS astronauts will do scientific experiments, observe the Earth and learn how to live in space.

Central truss

US laboratory

Japanese and European modules to be attached here

USA

The space shuttle

Most rockets can only be sent into space once, but the space shuttle can be launched again and again. It is used to ferry astronauts and cargo between the Earth and space.

Reusable spacecraft

The space shuttle blasts off from Kennedy Space Center in Florida, with the help of two rocket boosters and an external fuel tank. The boosters are filled with solid fuel, like huge fireworks. The fuel tank supplies liquid hydrogen and oxygen to three rocket engines in the spacecraft's tail. When the boosters and fuel tank are almost empty, they fall away. The boosters splash down in the Atlantic Ocean, where they are collected by ships to be used again. The fuel tank breaks up as it tumbles into the Indian Ocean, the only part of the system that cannot be used again. The orbiter spacecraft continues into space.

Working in space

In space, the orbiter's payload bay doors open. Inside, there may be a satellite to launch. Sometimes, shuttle astronauts have to work outside in space. They are either tethered to the orbiter by safety lines or they move freely using a gas-powered backpack.

Shuttle astronauts work in their shirt-sleeves inside the orbiter. Outside, they wear a protective spacesuit.

Return to Earth

At the end of its mission, the orbiter reenters the Earth's atmosphere. It glows white hot, but is protected by heat-resistant tiles. It glides on a zigzagging path to slow down. When it is just 89 feet (27 meters) above the ground, its wheels are lowered and it lands on a runway.

The space shuttle orbiter touches down at Kennedy Space Center.

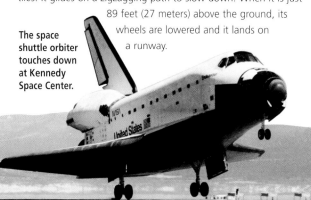

Space probes

Uncrewed spacecraft have crashed into, flown past, or orbited every planet in the solar system except Pluto. Their cameras and instruments have also probed moons, comets, and asteroids.

First steps to the planets

The first spacecraft to leave Earth's orbit and head out towards another world was *Luna 1*, launched toward the Moon by the Soviet Union in 1959. Over 30 U.S. Ranger and Surveyor probes and Soviet Luna probes followed it. The U.S. Mariner series of spacecraft flew past Mars, Venus, and Mercury. Soviet Venera craft landed on Venus and sent back the first photographs of its surface. In the early 1970s, *Pioneers 10* and *11* were the first space probes to cross the asteroid belt beyond Mars and fly past Jupiter.

Photographs taken by Soviet Venera probes show Venus's barren rocky surface.

Veneras 9 to *14* had two parts—an orbiter and a lander (pictured here) both carried television cameras.

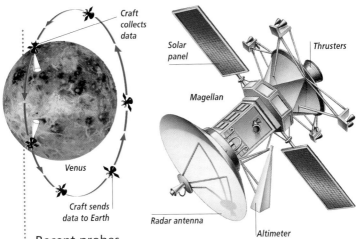

Craft collects data

Solar panel

Thrusters

Magellan

Venus

Radar antenna

Altimeter

Craft sends data to Earth

Recent probes

In the mid-1970s, the Viking probes landed on Mars. In the 1980s, *Giotto* flew past Halley's Comet. In the 1990s, *Magellan* used radar to create a detailed map of Venus, *Ulysses* flew over the Sun's poles, *Galileo* dropped a probe into Jupiter's atmosphere, *Lunar Prospector* collected data about the Moon's surface and *Pathfinder* landed a small rover vehicle, called *Sojourner*, on Mars.

Future explorers

In 2004, the *Cassini* space probe will reach Saturn after a six-year flight from Earth. It will release a smaller probe, *Huygens,* that will parachute into the atmosphere of Titan, Saturn's moon, taking measurements as it descends.

Artist's painting of *Huygens* parachuting towards Titan

Voyagers to the planets

The most successful space probes so far are the Voyager space probes. They made a grand tour of the outer planets in the 1970s and 1980s and sent back breathtaking, close-up photographs.

The Voyager missions

In 1977, *Voyager 1* and *Voyager 2* were launched toward the outer planets. They toured the solar system for 10 years, taking photographs and measurements all the way. Both of the Voyagers have now left the planets far behind and are heading toward the stars.

Voyagers 1 and *2* flew past Jupiter in 1979. They each took 17,000 photographs.

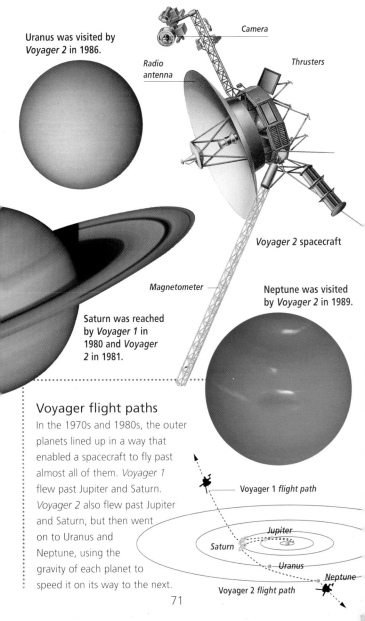

Uranus was visited by *Voyager 2* **in 1986.**

Camera

Radio antenna

Thrusters

Voyager 2 spacecraft

Magnetometer

Saturn was reached by *Voyager 1* **in 1980 and** *Voyager 2* **in 1981.**

Neptune was visited by *Voyager 2* **in 1989.**

Voyager flight paths

In the 1970s and 1980s, the outer planets lined up in a way that enabled a spacecraft to fly past almost all of them. *Voyager 1* flew past Jupiter and Saturn. *Voyager 2* also flew past Jupiter and Saturn, but then went on to Uranus and Neptune, using the gravity of each planet to speed it on its way to the next.

Voyager 1 *flight path*

Jupiter

Saturn

Uranus

Neptune

Voyager 2 *flight path*

71

Searching for other planets

The Earth is the only place in the universe where we know for sure that life exists. But are we really alone in the universe, or are there intelligent beings living on other planets?

The search for life

If there are planets orbiting other stars, they are so far away that they are too small for us to see, even with the most powerful telescopes. But a planet's gravity tugs a star as the planet orbits it, making the star wobble. Astronomers can detect this wobble.

Around 25 wobbling stars that we believe have planets orbiting them have been found so far. Most of them are giants, bigger than Jupiter.

Cloud of dust and gas around newly formed stars in the Orion Nebula

Some of the new stars in the Orion Nebula could have their own system of planets—home to other life.

72

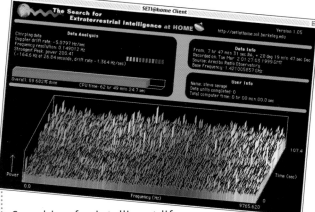

Searching for intelligent life

If there are planets orbiting other stars, then some of them may be home to intelligent beings. And if those beings are advanced, they probably use radio. The Search for Extraterrestrial Intelligence (SETI) involves analyzing radio signals from space.

The SETI at Home Project uses home computers to help analyse data from radio telescopes.

Alien encounters

Science fiction movies often feature alien creatures. Most of them look similar to humans, but computer-generated characters are now so realistic that they can be any shape and size and need not be limited by the need to fit a human actor inside a costume.

Could movie characters like Jabba the Hutt (left) from *Star Wars* actually exist on a distant planet?

Fact file

Aftermath of the explosion of Supernova 1987a captured in an X-ray image.

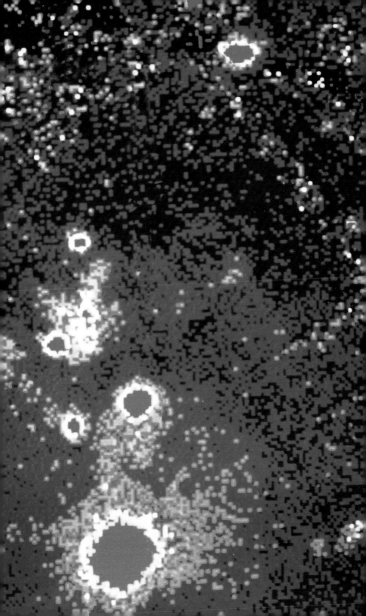

Star maps

The star maps on the following pages will help you to find your way around the night sky. They show the easiest of the 88 constellations to find.

Using the maps

Your view of the sky depends on the date, the time, and your latitude (how far north or south of the equator you are). Use this world map to find your latitude from the three bands shown (40°–60°N, 20°–40°N and 20°–40°S), then turn to the star maps for your latitude. Next, find the pair of maps for the right time of year. One shows the sky looking to the north; the other shows the sky looking to the south. The dates and times under each map show when it is exactly correct. Add one hour to the times shown during daylight saving time.

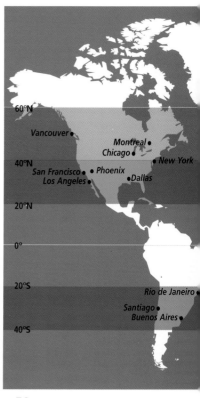

The night sky

As the Earth spins, the stars appear to move. Above the North Pole, they rotate around Polaris, the Pole Star (right). In the southern skies, they rotate around a point near the constellation Crux, the Southern Cross.

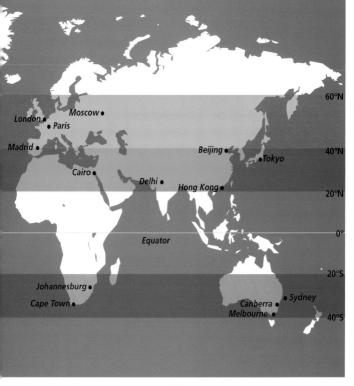

60°N

London •   Moscow •
   • Paris

Madrid •

40°N

Beijing •
   • Tokyo

Cairo •

Delhi •

Hong Kong •

20°N

Equator

0°

20°S

Johannesburg •

Cape Town •

Canberra •   • Sydney
Melbourne •

40°S

Star maps for latitudes 40° – 60°N

Winter sky
(north)

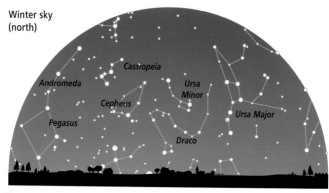

W   N   E

1 a.m., December 1
11 p.m., January 1
9 p.m., February 1

Winter sky
(south)

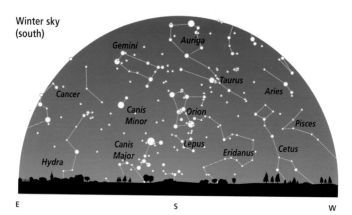

E   S   W

1 a.m., December 1
11 p.m., January 1
9 p.m., February 1

Star maps for latitudes 40° – 60°N

Spring sky
(north)

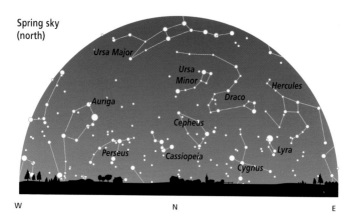

W   N   E

1 a.m., March 1
11 p.m., April 1
9 p.m., May 1

Spring sky
(south)

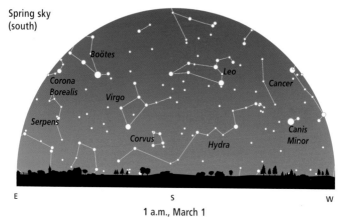

E   S   W

1 a.m., March 1
11 p.m., April 1
9 p.m., May 1

Star maps for latitudes 40° – 60°N

Summer sky (north)

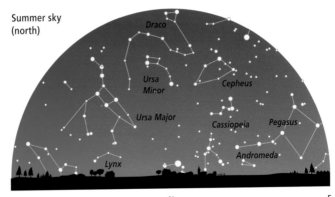

1 a.m., June 1
11 p.m., July 1
9 p.m., August 1

Summer sky (south)

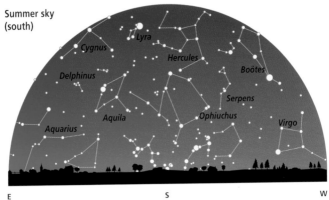

1 a.m., June 1
11 p.m., July 1
9 p.m., August 1

Star maps for latitudes 40° – 60°N

Fall sky
(north)

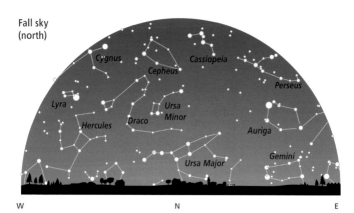

W   N   E

1 a.m., September 1
11 p.m., October 1
9 p.m., November 1

Fall sky
(south)

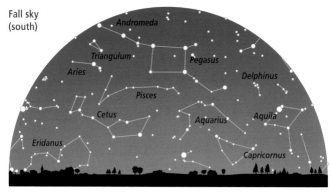

E   S   W

1 a.m., September 1
11 p.m., October 1
9 p.m., November 1

Star maps for latitudes 20° – 40°N

Winter sky (north)

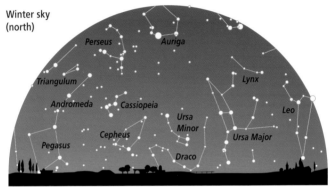

1 a.m., December 1
11 p.m., January 1
9 p.m., February 1

Winter sky (south)

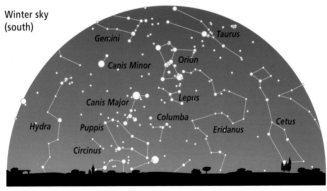

1 a.m., December 1
11 p.m., January 1
9 p.m., February 1

Star maps for latitudes 20° – 40°N

Spring sky
(north)

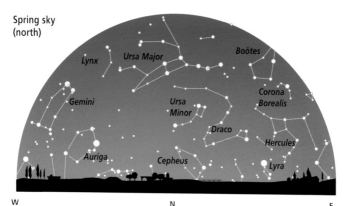

1 a.m., March 1
11 p.m., April 1
9 p.m., May 1

Spring sky
(south)

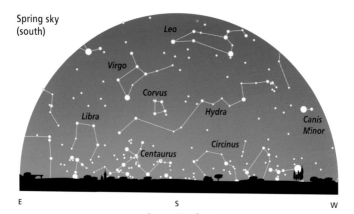

1 a.m., March 1
11 p.m., April 1
9 p.m., May 1

Star maps for latitudes 20° – 40°N

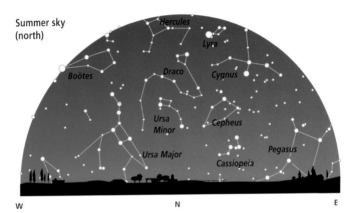

Summer sky
(north)

Hercules
Lyra
Boötes
Draco
Cygnus
Ursa Minor
Cepheus
Ursa Major
Pegasus
Cassiopeia

W   N   E

1 a.m., June 1
11 p.m., July 1
9 p.m., August 1

Summer sky
(south)

Ophiuchus
Serpens
Delphinus
Aquila
Virgo
Sagittarius
Scorpius
Libra
Aquarius
Capricornus

E   S   W

1 a.m., June 1
11 p.m., July1
9 p.m., August 1

Star maps for latitudes 20° – 40°N

Fall sky
(north)

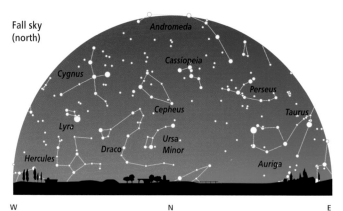

1 a.m., September 1
11 p.m., October 1
9 p.m., November 1

Fall sky
(south)

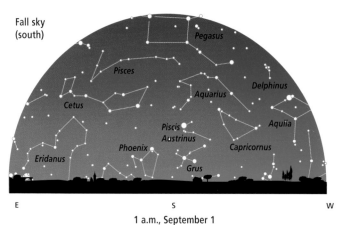

1 a.m., September 1
11 p.m., October 1
9 p.m., November 1

Star maps for latitudes 20° – 40°S

Summer sky
(north)

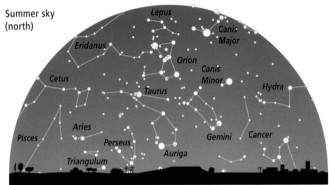

W   N   E

1 a.m., December 1
11 p.m., January 1
9 p.m., February 1

Summer sky
(south)

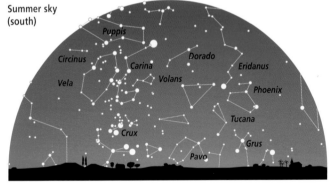

E   S   W

1 a.m., December 1
11 p.m., January 1
9 p.m., February 1

Star maps for latitudes 20° – 40°S

Fall sky
(north)

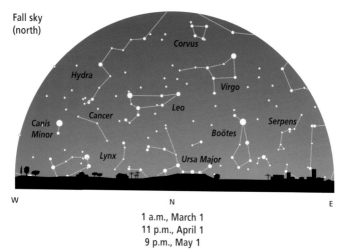

W   N   E

1 a.m., March 1
11 p.m., April 1
9 p.m., May 1

Fall sky
(south)

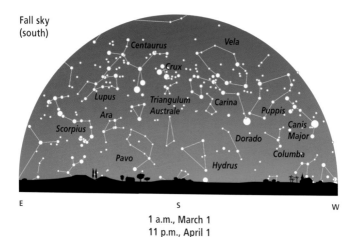

E   S   W

1 a.m., March 1
11 p.m., April 1
9 p.m., May 1

Star maps for latitudes 20° – 40°S

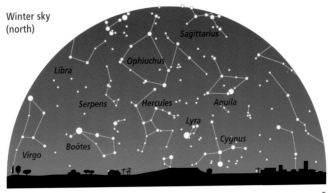

Winter sky (north)

1 a.m., June 1
11 p.m., July 1
9 p.m., August 1

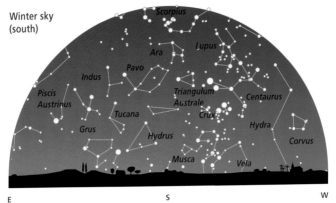

Winter sky (south)

1 a.m., June 1
11 p.m., July 1
9 p.m., August 1

Star maps for latitudes 20° – 40°S

Spring sky
(north)

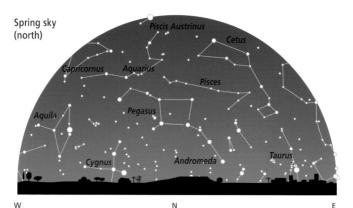

1 a.m., September 1
11 p.m., October 1
9 p.m., November 1

Spring sky
(south)

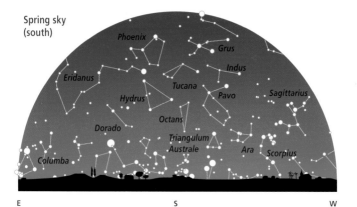

1 a.m., September 1
11 p.m., October 1
9 p.m., November 1

The Sun

The Sun contains more than 99 percent of the mass, or amount of matter, of the whole solar system. Its mass is the same as 330,000 Earths.

THE SUN

Distance from Earth: 92,960,000 miles (149,600,000 km)

Diameter: 864,000 miles (1,392,000 km)

Spin period: 36 days at poles; 25 days at equator

Earth
(to scale)

Solar Energy

Astronomers describe the Sun as a yellow dwarf because of its color and size. They also divide stars into groups, called spectral classes, according to their color and temperature. The Sun belongs to spectral class G2. It converts matter in its core into energy at the rate of 4.9 million tons (5 million tonnes) per second. It takes several hundred thousand years for this energy to travel out through the radiative zone and the convection zone before it reaches the surface and radiates away into space.

Photosphere

Convection zone

Radiative zone

Core

Solar and lunar eclipses

Astronomers know precisely how the Earth, Moon, and Sun move in relation to each other. Projecting their orbits into the future enables them to predict solar and lunar eclipses.

Total solar eclipses until 2005
June 21, 2001
December 4, 2002
November 23, 2003
April 8, 2005

Total lunar eclipses until 2005
January 21, 2000
July 16, 2000
January 9, 2001
May 16, 2003
November 9, 2003
May 4, 2004
October 28, 2004

Chromosphere

SOLAR SYSTEM FACT FILE

Planet	Average distance from Sun*	Mass (times Earth's mass)	Time taken to spin once on axis	Time taken to orbit Sun once (Earth days/years)
Mercury	0.387	0.055	58.65 Earth days	87.97 days
Venus	0.723	0.815	243.16 Earth days	224.70 days
Earth	1.0	1.0	23.93 hours	365.26 days
Mars	1.524	0.107	24.6 Earth hours	686.98 days
Jupiter	5.203	318	9.9 Earth hours	11.86 years
Saturn	9.539	95	10.5 Earth hours	29.46 years
Uranus	19.18	14.5	17.2 Earth hours	84.01 years
Neptune	30.06	17.2	16.1 Earth hours	164.8 years
Pluto	39.5	0.002	6.39 Earth days	247.7 years

* times Earth's average distance from Sun of 149.6 million km (92.9 million miles)

The planets

The following pages give information about the internal structure, distance from Earth, size, and temperature of the planets and the Moon.

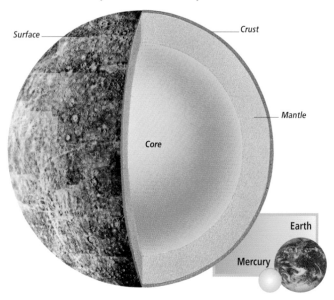

Surface

Crust

Mantle

Core

Earth

Mercury

MERCURY FACT FILE

Distance from Earth:
48.0 to 137.9 million miles
(77.3 to 221.9 million km)

Diameter at equator:
3,031 miles (4,878 km)

Average surface temperature:
–297°F (–183°C) to 800°F (427°C)

Mercury has no real atmosphere but the planet is surrounded by a tiny amount of gas, mostly made up of sodium and helium. Like the other rocky planets (Venus, Earth, and Mars) it is mostly made of rock and iron.

The *Magellan* space probe mapped Venus by using radar to cut through the planet's thick atmosphere. The colors were added by computer: yellow for highlands, and orange and brown for lowlands.

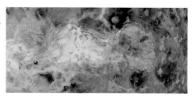

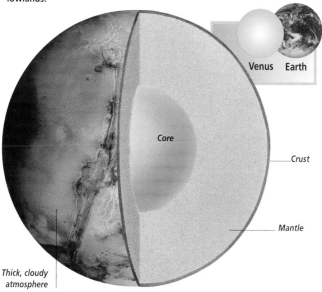

Venus   Earth

Core

Crust

Mantle

Thick, cloudy atmosphere

VENUS FACT FILE

Distance from Earth:
23.7 to 162.2 million miles
(38.2 to 261.0 million km)

Diameter at equator:
7,521 miles (12,104 km)

Average surface temperature:
896°F (480°C)

Venus has a thick atmosphere made up mainly of carbon dioxide (96%) with a small amount of nitrogen (3.5%) and other gases (0.5%). It has hundreds of thousands of volcanoes. Most are around 2 miles (3 kilometers) wide and 300 feet (90 meters) high.

Scarlet lava erupts from a volcano. Volcanoes move millions of tons (tonnes) of rock to the Earth's surface from its interior. Storms, floods, and earthquakes also help to reshape the planet.

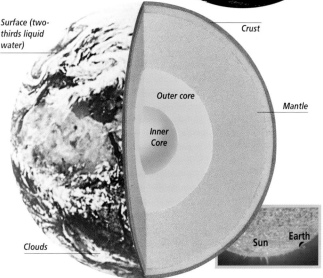

Surface (two-thirds liquid water)

Crust

Outer core

Mantle

Inner Core

Clouds

Sun   Earth

EARTH FACT FILE

Distance from Sun:
92.96 million miles
(149.6 million km)

Diameter at equator:
7,926 miles (12,756 km)

Average surface temperature:
57°F (14°C)

The Earth's surface crust floats on a hot rocky mantle that can flow like thick treacle. At the center of the Earth, a solid iron inner core is surrounded by a liquid iron outer core. Electric currents in the outer core produce the Earth's magnetic field.

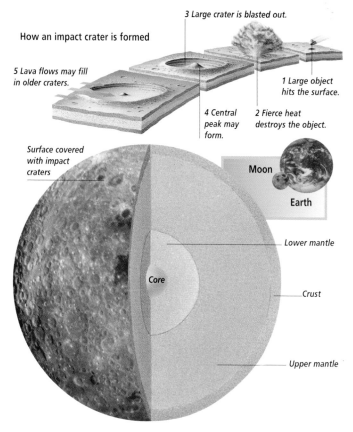

How an impact crater is formed

3 Large crater is blasted out.

5 Lava flows may fill in older craters.

4 Central peak may form.

1 Large object hits the surface.

2 Fierce heat destroys the object.

Surface covered with impact craters

Moon

Earth

Lower mantle

Core

Crust

Upper mantle

MOON FACT FILE

Distance from Earth:
238,903 miles (384,467 km)

Diameter at Equator:
2,160 miles (3,476 km)

Average surface temperature:
−300°F (−185°C) to 248°F (120°C)

Spin period: 27.32 Earth days

The Moon's interior is solid. Because there is no liquid core, there is no volcanic activity on the Moon. Instruments left on the Moon by the Apollo astronauts have recorded moonquakes, but they are 100 billion times less intense than earthquakes.

MOONS OF MARS

Mars has two rocky moons: Phobos and Deimos. Phobos measures 17 by 12 miles (28 by 20 km), while smaller Deimos is only 10 by 7 miles (16 by 12 km).

Deimos

Phobos

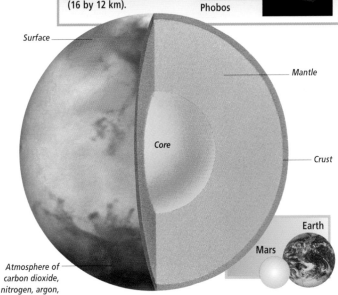

Surface

Mantle

Core

Crust

Earth

Mars

Atmosphere of carbon dioxide, nitrogen, argon, and other gases.

MARS FACT FILE

Distance from Earth:
33.9 to 249.4 million miles (54.5 to 401.3 million km)

Diameter at equator:
4,222 miles (6,794 km)

Average surface temperature:
−81°F (−63°C)

The atmosphere of Mars is 100 times thinner than that of Earth and is mainly made up of carbon dioxide gas (95.3%). Mars is the home of the solar system's biggest volcano, Olympus Mons, which stands 16 miles (25 kilometers) high.

Io's surface is covered in volcanoes that erupt with clouds of sulfur and sulfur dioxide. Plumes of gas can rise up to 185 miles (300 km) high.

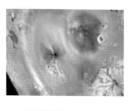

JUPITER'S MOONS*

Name	Diameter in miles (km)
Metis	12 (20)
Adrastea	25 (40)
Amalthea	125 (200)
Thebe	55 (90)
Io	2,256 (3,630)
Europa	1,950 (3,138)
Ganymede	3,270 (5,262)
Callisto	2,983 (4,800)
Leda	9 (15)
Himalia	112 (180)
Lysithea	25 (40)
Elara	50 (80)
Ananke	19 (30)
Carme	19 (30)
Pasiphae	22 (36)
Sinope	17 (28)

*from nearest to farthest from Jupiter

Liquid metallic hydrogen

Rocky core

Liquid hydrogen

Jupiter

Earth

Atmosphere of hydrogen and helium

JUPITER FACT FILE

Distance from Earth:
365.7 to 601.6 million miles
(588.5 to 968.1 million km)

Diameter at equator:
88,846 miles (142,984 km)

Temperature of cloud-tops:
−202°F (−130°C)

Jupiter's small rocky core is surrounded by hydrogen, which has been squashed by Jupiter's gravity into something that resembles a liquid metal. Clouds of frozen crystals of water, ammonia, and other chemicals float in its atmosphere of hydrogen and helium gas.

MOONS OF SATURN*

Moon	Diameter **	Moon	Diameter	Moon	Diameter
Pan	12 (20)	Mimas	245 (394)	Helene	19 (30)
Atlas	25 (40)	Enceladus	312 (502)	Rhea	951 (1,530)
Prometheus	62 (100)	Tethys	651 (1,048)	Titan	3,200 (5,150)
Pandora	55 (88)	Telesto	16 (25)	Hyperion	168 (270)
Epimetheus	75 (120)	Calypso	10 (16)	Iapetus	892 (1,435)
Janus	118 (190)	Dione	696 (1,120)	Phoebe	137 (220)

* From nearest to farthest from Saturn
** in miles (km)

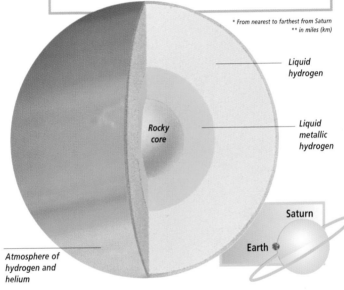

Liquid hydrogen

Liquid metallic hydrogen

Rocky core

Saturn

Earth

Atmosphere of hydrogen and helium

SATURN FACT FILE

Distance from Earth:
743.2 to 1,030.6 million miles
(1,195.5 to 1,658.5 million km)

Diameter at equator:
74,900 miles (120,536 km)

Temperature at cloud-tops:
−202°F (−130°C)

Saturn is a gas giant like Jupiter. Its internal structure is similar to that of Jupiter, with a tiny rocky core surrounded by hydrogen and helium. Saturn is the lightest planet in relation to its size.

MOONS OF URANUS*

Moon	Diameter**	Moon	Diameter	Moon	Diameter
Cordelia	16 (26)	Portia	67 (108)	Umbriel	726 (1,169)
Ophelia	19 (30)	Rosalind	34 (54)	Titania	980 (1,578)
Bianca	26 (42)	Belinda	41 (66)	Oberon	946 (1,523)
Cressida	39 (62)	Puck	96 (154)	S/1997 U2	100 (160)
Desdemona	34 (54)	Miranda	293 (472)	S/1997 U1	50 (80)
Juliet	52 (84)	Ariel	720 (1,158)	S/1986 U10	25 (40)

*From nearest to farthest from Uranus
** in miles (km)

Water, ice, methane, and ammonia

Rocky core

Atmosphere of hydrogen, helium, and methane

Clouds

Uranus

Earth

URANUS FACT FILE

Distance from Earth:
1,604.4 to 1,961.9 million miles
(2,581.9 to 3,157.3 million km)

Diameter at equator:
31,763 miles (51,118 km)

Temperature at cloud-tops:
–328°F (–200°C)

Uranus has a small, rocky core surrounded by hydrogen, helium, and methane. Because Uranus is tipped over, one pole is the warmest place on the planet for 42 years, while the other pole endures a 42-year winter.

NEPTUNE'S MOONS

Moon	Diameter**	Moon	Diameter
Naiad	34 (54)	Larissa	119 (192)
Thalassa	50 (80)	Proteus	258 (416)
Despina	112 (180)	Triton	1,681 (2,705)
Galatea	93 (150)	Nereid	149 (240)

*From nearest to farthest from Neptune   ** in miles (km)

Clouds on Neptune

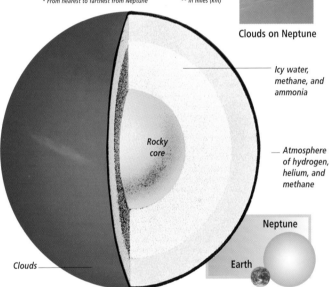

Icy water, methane, and ammonia

Rocky core

Atmosphere of hydrogen, helium, and methane

Neptune

Earth

Clouds

NEPTUNE FACT FILE

Distance from Earth:
2,675.6 to 2,912.6 million miles
(4,305.9 to 4,687.3 million km)

Diameter at equator:
30,779 miles (49,532 km)

Temperature at cloud-tops:
−328°F (−200°C)

Neptune has a very similar internal structure to Uranus, but unlike Uranus, heat rises from Neptune's core and drives weather systems in its atmosphere. Violent winds blow clouds around the planet at more than 620 miles per hour (1,000 kilometers per hour).

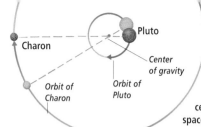

Pluto and Charon are so similar in size that they behave like a double planet. They orbit each other around their combined center of gravity—a point in space near Pluto.

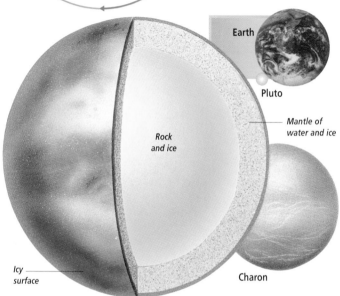

Earth

Pluto

Mantle of water and ice

Rock and ice

Icy surface

Charon

PLUTO FACT FILE

Distance from Earth:
2,668.1 to 4,681.1 million miles
(4,293.7 to 7,533.3 million km)

Diameter at equator:
1,413 miles (2,274 km)

Average surface temperature:
-373°F (-225°C)

Scientists think that Pluto may have a large core of rock covered with a layer of water ice 125–185 miles (200–300 kilometers) thick. On the surface, frozen methane, carbon monoxide, and nitrogen form a frosty layer several miles (kilometers) deep.

Asteroids, comets, and stars

On the following pages you will find facts, figures, and dates for a variety of space objects from asteroids and comets to meteors and stars.

ASTEROID FACT FILE

Name	Date discovered	Approximate diameter	Distance from Sun*
Ceres	1801	605 miles (975 km)	2.77
Pallas	1802	330 miles (535 km)	2.77
Vesta	1807	325 miles (525 km)	2.36
Hygeia	1849	265 miles (425 km)	3.14
Davida	1903	200 miles (325 km)	3.18
Interamnia	1910	200 miles (325 km)	3.06
Cybele	1861	175 miles (280 km)	3.43
Europa	1858	175 miles (280 km)	3.10
Sylvia	1866	170 miles (270 km)	3.49
Patientia	1899	170 miles (270 km)	3.06
Juno	1804	165 miles (265 km)	2.67
Psyche	1852	165 miles (265 km)	2.92
Euphrsyne	1854	155 miles (250 km)	3.15

* (Earth = 1)

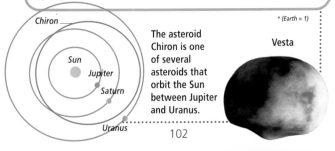

The asteroid Chiron is one of several asteroids that orbit the Sun between Jupiter and Uranus.

Vesta

A long period comet follows a long, wide orbit around the Sun. If it passes close to a large planet, it may be pulled into a new, tighter orbit and become a short period comet.

Orbit of a long period comet

Orbit of Neptune

Orbit of comet pulled into tight orbit around Jupiter

Sun

Orbit of Jupiter

Orbit of Halley's Comet (short period)

NOTABLE COMETS

Name	Date discovered	Description
Halley's Comet	1705	Has returned every 76 years since 240 B.C.
Lexell	1770	Closest comet to Earth, passed within 1.4 million miles (2.2 million km)
Encke's Comet	1786	Very short period comet—only 3.3 years
Great March Comet	1843	Had a giant tail 199 million miles (320 million km) long
Great Comet	1861	Spectacular fan-shaped tail
Swift-Tuttle	1862	Parent comet of the Perseid meteor shower
Arend-Roland	1956	Has an "anti-tail" that points towards Sun
Ikeya-Seki	1965	Bright sun-grazing comet, 880-year period
Bennett	1970	Dramatic curved tail and jets from nucleus
Kohoutek	1973	Photographed by Pioneer space probe
West	1975	Brightest comet since Ikeya-Seki
Shoemaker-Levy 9	1993	Broke up and collided with Jupiter (1994)
Hale-Bopp	1995	Visible to the naked eye in 1997
Hyakutake	1996	Brightest comet since West
Tabur	1996	Expected to be very bright, but faded

The Hoba West meteorite, the largest meteorite ever found on Earth, was discovered in Namibia in 1920. It weighs 121,250 lb (55,000 kg). It fell to Earth around 80,000 years ago.

METEOR SHOWER FACT FILE

Name	Date of maximum	Associated comet	Period
Quadrantids	January 3	-	-
Lyrids	April 21	1861 1	415 years
Eta Aquarids	May 4	Halley	76 years
Delta Aquarids	July 30	-	-
Perseids	August 11	Swift-Tuttle	105 years
Draconids	October 9	Giacobini-Zinner	7 years
Orionids	October 20	Halley	76 years
Taurids	October 31	Encke	3 years
Leonids	November 16	1866 I	33 years
Geminids	December 13	Phaethon (an asteroid)	1.4 years

NEAREST STARS TO EARTH

Name	Distance (light-years)	Name	Distance (light-years)
Proxima Centauri	4.3	Luyten 726-8	8.5
Alpha Centauri	4.4	Sirius	8.6
Barnard's Star	5.9	Ross 154	9.5
Wolf 359	7.7	Ross 248	10.2
Lalande 21185	8.2	Eta Eridani	10.7

DOUBLE AND MULTIPLE STARS

Name	Constellation	Description
Gamma Andromedae (Almaak)	Andromeda	Triple star
Epsilon Bootis (Izar)	Boötes	Double star
Alpha Capricorni	Capricornus	Two binary stars
Beta Cephei (Alphirk)	Cepheus	Variable binary
Alpha Centauri	Centaurus	Closest binary to the Sun
Beta Cygni (Albireo)	Cygnus	Blue/gold double
Alpha Geminorum (Castor)	Gemini	Three binaries
Delta Gruis	Grus	Naked-eye double
Alpha Librae (Zuben el Genubi)	Libra	Double star
Zeta Ursae Majoris (Mizar/Alcor)	Ursa Major	Double star

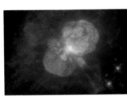

Eta Carinae was as bright as Sirius in 1843, but is now too dim to see without binoculars.

VARIABLE STARS

Star	Period (days)
Eta Aquilae	7.2
R Carinae	308.7
R Centauri	546.2
Delta Cephei	5.4
Omicron Ceti	332

BRIGHTEST STARS

Star	Distance (light-years)	Magnitude
Sirius	8.8	−1.5
Canopus	98	−0.7
Alpha Centauri	4.4	−0.3
Arcturus	36	0.0
Vega	26	0.0
Capella	46	0.1
Rigel	815	0.1
Procyon	11.4	0.4
Betelgeuse	489	0.5
Achernar	65	0.5
Hadar	525	0.6
Altair	16.6	0.8

Crewed spacecraft

The first crewed spacecraft were tiny, cramped one-person capsules. Apollo spacecraft took three astronauts to the Moon. Today, the space shuttle carries crews of up to seven.

VOSTOK, VOSHKOD, AND SOYUZ MISSIONS

Name	Launched	Crew	Orbits	Description
Vostok 1	4-12-61	Yuri Gagarin	1	First manned spaceflight
Vostok 3	8-11-62	Andrian Nikolayev	64	First double flight (with Vostok 4)
Vostok 6	6-16-63	Valentina Tereshkova	48	First woman in space
Voshkod 1	10-12-64	Vladimir Komarov Konstantin Feoktistov Boris Yegorov	16	First three-man spaceflight
Voshkod 2	3-1-65	Pavel Belyayev, Alexei Leonov	17	First spacewalk (by Leonov)
Soyuz 1	4-23-67	Vladimir Shatalov	48	First Soyuz flight
Soyuz 4	1-14-69	Vladimir Shatalov	30	First docking of two spacecraft (with Soyuz 5)

Vostok capsule

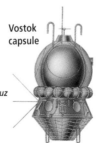

Soyuz capsule

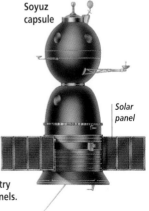

Solar panel

Vostok and Soyuz launch rockets have a central core surrounded by extra booster rockets.

Vostok was a tiny one-person capsule. Soyuz carries three crew members and have orbital and reentry modules and solar panels.

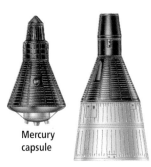

Mercury capsule

Gemini capsule

Atlas rockets launched four Mercury capsules, each carrying one astronaut. Heavier Gemini craft carrying two crew members needed the more powerful Titan rocket.

Titan

Atlas

MAIN MERCURY AND GEMINI MISSIONS

Name	Launched	Crew	Orbits	Description
Mercury 3	5-5-61	Alan Shepard	Sub-orbital	First American astronaut
Mercuty 6	2-20-62	John Glenn	3	First American in orbit
Gemini 4	6-3-65	McDivitt, White	62	First U.S. spacewalk (by White)
Gemini 8	3-16-66	Armstrong, Scott	6	First U.S. docking

Apollo

Lunar module

Command module

Service module

Saturn 5 rocket

The 49-ton (50-tonne) Apollo spacecraft was launched by the Saturn Moon rocket.

APOLLO MISSIONS

Name	Launched	Crew
Apollo 8	12-21-68	Borman, Lovell, Anders
Apollo 9	3-3-69	McDivitt, Scott, Schweickart
Apollo 10	5-18-69	Stafford, Cernan, Young
Apollo 11	7-16-69	Armstrong, Aldrin, Collins
Apollo 12	11-12-69	Conrad, Gordon, Bean
Apollo 13	4-11-60	Lovell, Swigert, Haise
Apollo 14	1-31-71	Shepard, Roosa, Mitchell
Apollo 15	7-26-71	Scott, Irwin, Worden
Apollo 16	4-16-72	Young, Mattingly, Duke
Apollo 17	12-7-72	Cernan, Evans, Schmitt

The space shuttle

A fleet of space shuttles have been flying to and from space since 1981. They have launched satellites and space probes and have carried space laboratories into orbit.

SPACE SHUTTLES

Orbiter	Maiden flight	Firsts
Columbia	4-12-81	First space shuttle mission (4-12-81)
Challenger	4-4-83	-
Discovery	8-30–84	First docking with *International Space Station* (5-27-99)
Atlantis	10-3-85	First docking with *Mir* space station (6-27-95)
Endeavor	5-7-92	

Inside the orbiter

During a space shuttle mission, astronauts live and work on three decks in the orbiter's nose. The spacecraft is controlled from the flight deck at the top. Below, the mid-deck contains seating, a living area, the galley (kitchen), sleeping compartments, the toilet, equipment racks, and an airlock to give access to the payload bay. Below the mid-deck, the lower deck contains environmental control systems.

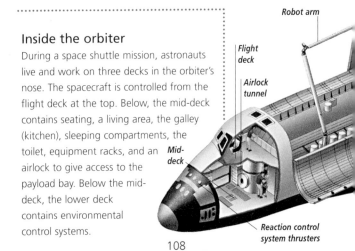

Robot arm

Flight deck

Airlock tunnel

Mid-deck

Reaction control system thrusters

NOTABLE SHUTTLE MISSIONS

Orbiter	Date	Description
Columbia	11-28-83	Carried *Spacelab-1* manned laboratory into orbit
Challenger	1-28-86	Orbiter broke up during launch; all seven crew killed
Atlantis	5-4-89	Launched *Magellan* probe to Venus
Atlantis	10-18-89	Launched *Galileo* probe to Jupiter
Discovery	4-25-90	Launched *Hubble Space Telescope*
Discovery	10-29-98	Mercury astronaut John Glenn returns to space
Endeavor	12-4-98	Launched *Unity,* second part of the *ISS*
Columbia	7-22-99	Launched *Chandra X-Ray Telescope*

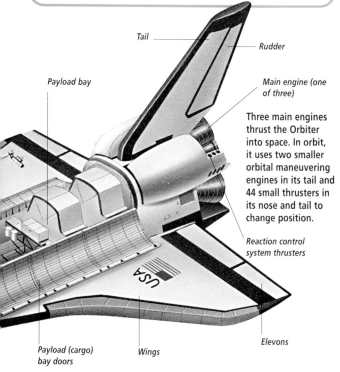

Tail

Rudder

Payload bay

Main engine (one of three)

Three main engines thrust the Orbiter into space. In orbit, it uses two smaller orbital maneuvering engines in its tail and 44 small thrusters in its nose and tail to change position.

Reaction control system thrusters

USA

Payload (cargo) bay doors

Wings

Elevons

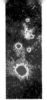

Space probes

Robot explorers carry cameras and other instruments across the solar system to study the planets, and their moons.

Lunar Prospector discovered billions of tons (tonnes) of ice in permanently shadowed craters at the lunar poles.

PROBES TO THE MOON

Probe	Launched	Country	Description
Luna 1	1-2-59	U.S.S.R.	First spacecraft to escape Earth orbit
Luna 2	9-12-59	U.S.S.R.	First spacecraft to hit the Moon
Surveyor 1	6-1-66	U.S.A.	First soft landing on the Moon
Luna 17	11-10-70	U.S.S.R.	Carried Lonokhod 1 robot to Moon
Luna Prospector	1-6-98	U.S.A.	Discovered water on the Moon

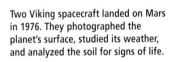

Two Viking spacecraft landed on Mars in 1976. They photographed the planet's surface, studied its weather, and analyzed the soil for signs of life.

PROBES TO MARS

Probe	Launched	Country	Description
Mariner 9	5-30-71	U.S.A.	Mapped Mars
Viking 1	8-20-75	U.S.A.	Landed on Mars
Viking 2	9-9-75	U.S.A.	Landed on Mars
Pathfinder	12-4-96	U.S.A.	Analyzed rocks on Mars
Global Surveyor	11-7-96	U.S.A.	Mapped Mars

PROBES TO MERCURY AND VENUS

Probe	Launched	Country	Description
Venera 3	11-16-65	U.S.S.R.	First spacecraft to hit Venus
Venera 7	8-17-70	U.S.S.R.	First soft landing on Venus
Mariner 10	11-3-73	U.S.A.	Flew past Mercury and Venus
Magellan	5-4-89	U.S.A.	Mapped Venus by radar

Mariner 10 measured Mercury's temperature and detected its magnetic field.

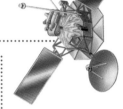

The *Cassini* spacecraft should reach Saturn in 2004.

THE GIANT PLANETS

Probe	Launched	Country	Description
Voyager 1	9-5-77	U.S.A.	Flew by Jupiter and Saturn
Voyager 2	8-20-77	U.S.A.	Toured the outer planets
Galileo	10-18-89	U.S.A.	Studied Jupiter
Cassini-Huygens	10-15-97	U.S.A./Europe	To study Saturn

Ulysses (left) orbited the Sun's poles. The *Near Earth Asteroid Rendezvous (NEAR)* spacecraft will study asteroids.

OTHER PROBES

Probe	Launched	Country	Description
Giotto	7-2-85	Europe	Studied Halley's Comet
Ulysses	10-6-90	Europe	Studied the Sun and the solar wind
NEAR	2-17-96	U.S.A.	Asteroid probe

Glossary

asteroid One of the millions of pieces of rock that orbit the Sun, especially in the asteroid belt between the orbits of Mars and Jupiter. Asteroids are also called minor planets.

astronaut Someone who travels into space. Travelers on Soviet or Russian rockets are called cosmonauts.

astronomer Someone who studies astronomy—the study of the universe and everything in it.

atmosphere The layer of gas that surrounds a planet, moon, or star.

atom A particle of matter, once thought to be the smallest possible particle of matter but now known to be made up of even smaller particles.

axis Imaginary line around which a planet, or another spinning object, rotates.

billion One thousand million.

black hole The collapsed core of a massive star with such strong gravity that nothing can escape from it—not even light.

chromosphere The part of the Sun's atmosphere that lies above the photosphere and below the corona.

cluster A family of stars or galaxies, held together by their force of gravity.

comet A piece of rock and snow in orbit around the Sun. As it nears the Sun, gas and vapor driven off by the Sun's warmth form one or more bright tails.

constellation One of 88 recognizable groups, or patterns, of stars seen in the night sky from Earth.

core The center of a moon, planet, star, or galaxy.

corona The outermost layer of the Sun's atmosphere.

crater A hollow or depression in the surface of a planet or moon caused by a meteorite hitting it.

crust The thin, rocky surface of a planet or moon.

double star Two stars that look close together, but are merely in the same direction when seen from Earth.

element A material in its simplest form, such as hydrogen. Elements make up all the matter in the universe, combining to form compounds. For example, carbon and oxygen form carbon dioxide.

equator An imaginary line around the Earth's middle, halfway between the North and South poles.

event horizon An imaginary boundary around a black hole. Inside it, the black hole's gravity is so strong that no matter or energy, including light, can escape from it.

galaxy Billions of stars moving through space, held together by gravity.

gamma rays A form of energy, like light, ultraviolet rays, and X-rays, but made from shorter waves and more powerful.

gravity A force of attraction between objects. The greater their mass (the amount of material they contain) and the closer they are to each other, the greater is the force of gravity pulling them together.

heat shield A thick covering that protects a spacecraft and its crew from the intense heat of reentry into the Earth's atmosphere.

helium The second most common element in the universe after hydrogen.

hydrogen The simplest, lightest, and most common element in the universe. Young stars are made almost entirely of hydrogen. Clouds of hydrogen swirl through the space between the stars.

infrared A kind of energy, like light, but made from longer waves beyond the red end of the rainbow. We cannot see infrared rays but we can feel them as warmth on our skin.

lander A spacecraft, or part of a spacecraft, that lands on a planet or a moon.

light Energy that travels through space in waves of electricity and magnetism called electromagnetic waves. We can see light, but not other electromagnetic waves, such as ultraviolet. White light is made of different colors, each with a different wavelength. Red waves are the longest; violet the shortest.

light-year The distance a ray of light travels in one year, used to measure vast distances in space between stars and galaxies. Light travels at 186,287 miles (299,792 kilometers) per second. In one year, light travels 5,900,000,000,000 miles (9,500,000,000,000 km). We call this distance a light-year.

magnetic field A region of space where magnetic forces can be detected.

magnitude Scale used to measure the brightness of a star or another object in the night sky. The brightest stars are magnitude 0 or −1. From Earth, we can see stars to about magnitude 6 with the naked eye.

mantle The part of a planet or moon that lies between its central core and crust.

mass The amount of matter, or material, in an object.

matter The material (solid, liquid, or gas) that everything in the universe is made from.

meteor The trail of light produced by a meteoroid as it burns up in the Earth's atmosphere. Also called a shooting star.

meteorite A meteor that lands on a planet or moon.

meteoroid A piece of rock or dust in the solar system.

"M" numbers Numbers used to name galaxies or clusters in space, taken from a list put together by 18th-century French astronomer Charles Messier.

moon A natural satellite of a planet.

nebula (plural **nebulae**) A cloud of gas and dust (mainly hydrogen) in space.

neutron star The remains of a collapsed star, made from matter compressed so much that it is made entirely from particles called neutrons.

nuclear energy Energy that can be released from the particles making up all matter.

nuclear fusion The process that goes on in the center of a star when atomic nuclei of one element, hydrogen, smash together and form a new element, helium, and release energy. Big, old stars go on to make heavier elements from helium when they have no hydrogen left.

nucleus (plural **nuclei**) The very center of something, especially of an atom, comet or galaxy.

observatory Place where astronomers use telescopes to study the stars.

orbit The endless path of one object around another object, the two held together by gravity: for example, a moon around a planet or a planet around a star.

orbiter A spacecraft or part of a spacecraft that orbits a star, planet, or moon.

particle A very small piece of matter.

photosphere The visible surface of the Sun.

planet A large object in orbit around the Sun or another star that does not give out light of its own.

planetary nebula A ring of gas thrown off by a dying star.

poles Points at opposite ends of a planet or moon (the north pole and south pole) joined by an imaginary line called an axis. The planet or moon rotates around its axis.

radiation Beams of energy, such as visible light or radio waves.

radio waves A form of energy that can travel through space and is invisible; similar to light but made from longer waves.

reentry The journey back into the Earth's atmosphere made by a spacecraft returning from space.

satellite An object that orbits a planet or a moon. A moon is a natural satellite. A spacecraft is an artificial (manmade) satellite.

shooting star Another name for a meteor.

solar wind Particles and radiation that flow away from the Sun into space.

space probe A spacecraft sent to study the Sun, a planet, a moon, or space itself.

spacewalk Time spent by an astronaut or cosmonaut in space outside his or her spacecraft. Also called extra-vehicular activity (EVA).

spicule A spike of hot gases shooting thousands of miles (kilometers) above the Sun's surface.

supernova (plural **supernovae**) A massive star that has exploded, sending clouds of gas and dust out into the surrounding space.

thrust The pushing force produced by a rocket engine.

thruster A small rocket engine or gas jet used to change a spacecraft's position.

ultraviolet Invisible electromagnetic waves similar to light but made from shorter waves beyond the violet end of the rainbow. Ultraviolet energy is given off by very hot objects, such as stars. The Sun gives out ultraviolet energy. It can harm living things, but most of it is stopped by the Earth's atmosphere.

X-rays Invisible energy waves that are similar to light but made from much shorter waves—shorter than ultraviolet waves. X-rays can pass through some materials. They are used in medicine to make images of bones through skin and muscle.

Index

Web sites

Note: Web sites are constantly being expanded and updated.

SPACE AGENCIES
http://www.nasa.com
NASA (the U.S. space agency) home page
http://www.jpl.nasa.gov
Jet Propulsion Labs (operates NASA's interplanetary space probes)
http://www.esa.int
The European Space Agency
http://www.arianespace.com
Arianespace home page (operates Ariane rockets)

TELESCOPES
http://www2.keck.hawaii.edu
Keck telescope in Hawaii
http://www.ifa.hawaii.edu/mko
Mauna Kea astronomical observatories
http://ngst.gsfc.nasa.gov
Next Generation Space Telescope data
http://www.jb.man.ac.uk
Jodrell Bank radio telescope (England) home page

MUSEUMS
http://www.cyberspacemuseum.com
(click on space places) Database giving U.S. museum information with access to other online space museum web sites

http://www.nasm.si.edu
Home page of the Smithsonian National Air and Space Museum, Washington, U.S.A.
http://www.nmsi.ac.uk
Home page of the Science Museum, London, England
http://www.rognmn.ac.uk
Home page of the Royal Observatory, Greenwich, England
http://www.bnsc.gov.uk
Home page of the British National Space Centre, London, England
http://www.nssc.co.uk
Home page of the National Space Science Centre, Leicester, England

FACTS
http://www.earthview.com/timetable/tenyear.htm
Future eclipse dates
http://comets.amsmeteors.org
Information on meteors
http://www.nssdc.gsfc.nasa.gov/planetary/factsheet
NASA factsheets on the Sun and planets
http://mars.jpl.nasa.gov
NASA Mars data

setiathome.ssl.berkeley.edu
SETI@home page
For infomation and to download free program to analyze radio telescope data at home

....

Acknowledgements

l = left; r = right; b = bottom; t = top; c = center

ILLUSTRATIONS

Mark Franklin, 60–61, 62 (br), 106–107; **Gary Hinks**, 32b; **Rob Jakeway**, 8–9, 10–11tl & b, 18–19b, 22–23, 27b, 28b, 32–33, 46–47, 48–49c, 50–51 (main image), 58, 59t, 63b; **Mainline Design**, 12r, 16, 44bl, 45tr, 55br, 63c, 95t ; **Peter Sarson**, 13t, 15, 31, 42, 56tr, 69t, 71br; **Guy Smith**, 11t & c, 17, 30b, 38–39, 43tr, 54l, 60l, 71tr, 90–91, 92, 93, 94, 95, 96, 97, 98, 99, 100, 101, 108–109, 110–111; **Roger Stewart**, 29t, 39br, 40–41, 48bl, 49br, 102bl; **Wil Tirion**, 43b, 76–77, 78–79, 80–81, 82–83, 84–85, 86–87, 88–89.

PHOTOGRAPHS

Ariane 503 Photogallery, 61t; **David P. Anderson, SMU/Science Photo Library**, 13; **Californian Institute of Technology + Carnegie Institution of Washington**, 41; **Corbis**, 11, 56–57 (background); **Digital Vision**, 17, 18t, 20, 21t, 21b, 30–31, 34–35, 37, 51t, 56t, 56b, 57t, 57b, 74–75, 77, 93t, 93b, 94b, 95, 96b, 100b; **European Space Agency/Science Photo Library**, 30; **JPL/NASA**, 27b; **Lick Observatory/NASA**, 16; **Star Wars: Episode I – the Phantom Menace ©1999 Lucasfilm Ltd. & TM. Courtesy of Lucasfilm Ltd.**, 73; **David Malin/Royal Observatory Edinburgh**, 39; **David Malin/Anglo-Australian Observatory**, 44; **NASA**, 6–7, 12, 18b, 19t, 19b, 20–21, 23t, 23b, 24, 25t, 25b, 26, 27t, 29, 36, 45, 46, 49, 51b, 52–53, 59, 63l, 63t, 64–65 (background), 65b, 66, 67t, 67c, 67b, 68, 69, 70, 70–71, 71l, 71r, 72, 92, 97t, 97b, 98, 99, 100t, 101, 102, 105; **NASA/ESA**, 28; **NASA/Science Photo Library**, 65t, 96t, 96tr; **The Natural History Museum, London**, 33l, 33r, 104; **NOAO/Science Photo Library**, 32–33; **Novosti**, 61b, 62t; **Novosti/Science Photo Library**, 62b; **Pekka Parviainen/Science Photo Library**, 31; **F. Salmoiraghi/Zefa-Stockmarket**, 94t; **John Sanford/Science Photo Library**, 54–55 (background), 55; **The Stock Market**, 14b, **Tony Stone Images**, 14t, 14–15 (background); **Frank Zullo/Science Photo Library**, 42.

COVER PHOTOGRAPHY/ARTWORK

Front l Science Photo Library, r Digital Vision; back Digital Vision.